The CHATELAINE DAYBOOK

2000

The CHATELAINE DAYBOOK

The Canadian Women's Engagement Calendar 2000

CHATELAINE

KEY PORTER BOOKS

ISBN: 1-55013-965-7

THE CANADA COUNCIL | LE CONSEIL DES ARTS
FOR THE ARTS | DU CANADA
SINCE 1957 | DEPUIS 1957

The publisher gratefully acknowledges the support of the Canada Council for the Arts and the Ontario Arts Council for its publishing program.

We also acknowledge the financial support of the Government of Canada through the Book Publishing Industry Development Program for our publishing activities.

Page 33, "Halos for Husbands" advertisement, courtesy Northern Telecom; page 51, photograph of Elizabeth Arden, courtesy Elizabeth Arden Canada; page 116, illustration December 1932 © Jack Keay. Reprinted by the kind permission of the artist.

Key Porter Books Limited
70 The Esplanade
Toronto, Ontario
Canada M5E 1R2
www.keyporter.com

Design: Tania Craan

Printed and bound in Canada

Introduction

It is with great pride that we present to you the first edition of *The Chatelaine Daybook: The Canadian Women's Engagement Calendar.* And what better way to introduce a calendar than by starting off in the year 2000? As we embark on this new century, *The Chatelaine Daybook* celebrates the history of Canadian women from the early years of the magazine (the early 20th century) to the present day, thus serving as a reminder of both how far we've come and how little we've changed. As you leaf through these pages, you'll see how many of the words written during the 20s, 30s and 40s could just as easily have been written today.

For over seventy years, *Chatelaine* magazine has sat side by side with its readers: applauding their successes and reflecting their thoughts and feelings. We hope that *The Chatelaine Daybook* will also be your daily companion as you make your way through yet another busy year in your life.

Chatelaine

The Canadian Woman's Magazine

JANUARY, 1946 • 10¢

			JANUARY			
S	M	T	W	T	F	S
						1
2	3	4	5	6	7	8
9	10	11	12	13	14	15
16	17	18	19	20	21	22
23	24	25	26	27	28	29
30	31					

4

December/January

MONDAY

27

TUESDAY

28

WEDNESDAY

29

THURSDAY

30

FRIDAY

31 New Year's Eve

SATURDAY

1 New Year's Day

SUNDAY

2

January

MONDAY

3   d.1963 Dorothy Sproule, poet and winner of the Coronation Medal in 1937

TUESDAY

4

WEDNESDAY

5   d.1987 Margaret Laurence, author

THURSDAY ●

6   b.1893 Madge Thurlow Macklin, pioneer researcher in the inheritance of disease

FRIDAY

7   d.1958 Margaret Anglin, actress

SATURDAY

8

SUNDAY

9   b.1802 Catharine Parr Traill, author

March 1928 issue

HOW *CHATELAINE* GOT ITS NAME

Over 75,000 suggestions flooded into the *Maclean's* offices after the announcement of a contest to name a new national women's magazine. Suggestions included Canadian Womanhood, Woman's Realm and Eve's Sphere. The winner was The Chatelaine, suggested by Hilda Pain, a rancher from Eburne, British Columbia, for a $1,000 prize. The name came from the chatelaine of the house whose job it was, as the lady of the château, to carry a ring of keys unlocking each door in the house.

JANUARY

S	M	T	W	T	F	S
						1
2	3	4	5	6	7	8
9	10	11	12	13	14	15
16	17	18	19	20	21	22
23	24	25	26	27	28	29
30	31					

January

MONDAY

10

TUESDAY

11

WEDNESDAY

12
1971 Dauphin, Manitoba, ends its tradition of firing female civic employees when they marry

THURSDAY

13

FRIDAY ◑

14
d.1968 Florence Wyle, sculptor

SATURDAY

15
b.1879 Mazo de la Roche, author

SUNDAY

16

August 1932 issue

A STITCH IN TIME

It wasn't so very long ago that every woman had a dress-maker, or knew how to sew. *Chatelaine* Patterns were available by mail order—allowing women in even the most remote rural areas to appear in the most up-to-date fashions. Patterns were available for business wear, evening apparel, house-dresses, children's clothing, and even lingerie.

January

MONDAY

17

TUESDAY

18 b.1913 Gwethalyn Graham, author

WEDNESDAY

19 b.1859 Alice Eastwood, Canadian botanist who rebuilt the California Academy of Sciences after the 1906 earthquake

THURSDAY ○

20 d.1989 Bea Lillie, comedienne

FRIDAY

21 d.1921 Beatrice La Palme, opera singer

SATURDAY

22 1992 Roberta Bondar blasts off and becomes the first Canadian woman in space

SUNDAY

23

September 1928 issue

ATHLETIC MAIDS TO ARMS!

In the 1930s the idea of women playing sports was highly controversial. Advocates claimed the "modern girl" was a healthier, happier woman for her fitness. However, naysayers denounced female athletes as unfeminine: "leather-legged, flat-chested muscle molls running around in sweater and shorts, feebly participating in events of athletic prowess that were woeful to watch," was how one journalist described them in 1933. Fortunately, most criticism fell on deaf ears. At the 1932 Los Angeles Olympic Games women set new world's records in the following sports: 100 metres—11.9 seconds by Stella Walsh; 80 metre hurdles—11.7 seconds, and javelin throwing—143 feet 4 inches by "Babe" Didrikson; and high jump—5 feet 5 3/4 inches by Jean Shiley.

JANUARY

S	M	T	W	T	F	S
						1
2	3	4	5	6	7	8
9	10	11	12	13	14	15
16	17	18	19	20	21	22
23	24	25	26	27	28	29
30	31					

January

MONDAY

24

TUESDAY

25 d.1975 Charlotte Whitton, first woman mayor of Ottawa

WEDNESDAY

26 d.1993 Jeanne Sauvé, first woman governor-general

THURSDAY

27

FRIDAY ◑

28

SATURDAY

29 1916 Manitoba becomes the first province to extend the vote to women

SUNDAY

30

March 1946 issue

FLIRTATIOUS FASHION

The bare bosom look, reminiscent of the feminine Edwardian era, and achieved this season in new boat neck-lines and strapless evening gowns, demands a dazzle of jew-ellery against the dazzle of skin! Jewellers have willingly complied with rhinestones that are big co-starring with silver, gold and pearls in dangling earrings, chokers, neck-laces, brooches and clips.

from "Fashion Shorts," December 1946

JANUARY

S	M	T	W	T	F	S
						1
2	3	4	5	6	7	8
9	10	11	12	13	14	15
16	17	18	19	20	21	22
23	24	25	26	27	28	29
30	31					

January/February

MONDAY	
31	
TUESDAY	
1	
WEDNESDAY	
2	
THURSDAY	
3	
FRIDAY	
4	b.1885 Cairine Reay Wilson, first woman appointed to the Canadian Senate
SATURDAY ●	
5	d.1968 Frances Loring, sculptor and chief organizer of the National Arts Council
SUNDAY	
6	

May 1933 issue

CAIRINE REAY WILSON
The First Female Senator

Mrs. Wilson was appointed Canada's first woman senator in 1930 by Prime Minister Mackenzie King. Mrs. Wilson's appointment was the first of its kind following the British Privy Council's ruling in the "Persons" case, which made it possible for women to hold the highest political office in the country. As a senator, Mrs. Wilson championed such issues as divorce and immigration, prompting *Chatelaine* to claim her as an important mentor for young Canadian women. In addition to her political talents, Senator Wilson also boasted superior qualities as a charming town-bred hostess and the always well-turned-out mother of eight.

FEBRUARY

S	M	T	W	T	F	S
				1	2	3	4	5
6	7	8	9	10	11	12
13	14	15	16	17	18	19
20	21	22	23	24	25	26
27	28	29				

FEBRUARY						
S	M	T	W	T	F	S
		1	2	3	4	5
6	7	8	9	10	11	12
13	14	15	16	17	18	19
20	21	22	23	24	25	26
27	28	29				

FEBRUARY

MONDAY

7

TUESDAY

8

WEDNESDAY

9

THURSDAY

10

FRIDAY

11

SATURDAY ◑

12 d.1954 Agnes MacPhail, first woman MPP

SUNDAY

13 b.1903 Elizabeth Homer Morton, founder of the Canadian Library Association

FEBRUARY

MONDAY	
14	St. Valentine's Day
TUESDAY	
15	1930 Cairine Reay Wilson is appointed to the Canadian Senate
WEDNESDAY	
16	
THURSDAY	
17	
FRIDAY	
18	
SATURDAY ○	
19	
SUNDAY	
20	b.1924 Evelyn C. Pielou, inventor of mathematical ecology

July 1929 issue

CHANGING SILHOUETTES

The present-day urge for the preservation of youth has turned our attention to plastic surgery as a means to an end. Many doctors are accumulating much largesse by lifting the sagging skin of the face and neck to restore youthful contour.

To most of us there is something distasteful about restoring or preserving a youthful appearance by such means. I saw a woman in Chicago who had undergone this treatment for her face and while it had unmistakably banished all look of age, it had also dispelled all expression, and made her look like a Benda mask.

from "The Promise of Beauty" by MAB, November 1929

A Fine Romance

THE BOOK OF LOVE

Love was in the air every month in the early years of *Chatelaine*. Fiction features were often of a romantic nature, varying from the banal girl-meets-boy, girl-marries-boy variety to melodramatic, illicit love affairs.

Fictional heroines were the ideal, and regular "how-to" style articles were brimming with practical advice for the reader who wished to be swept away by Mr. Tall, Dark and Handsome. A 1938 article advised women to be specific with their dates, asking questions that related to his leisure or professional life, questions like, "Do you really enjoy cutting up frogs?" if he was a scientist. Adding a touch of the little woman was also wise; "petrified of fast driving, thunderstorms and roller-coasters" encouraged men to act protective of women.

Advertisers also made use of the "get married" bandwagon. Many advised that use of their products would lead to a speedier trip down the aisle; washing clothes with Lux, deodorizing with Odorono, brushing with Colgate and using Tangee lipstick were all sure-fire ways to snag a man.

from "Why they elope," March 1929 issue
An only son just quietly married without saying a word to his parents…

TO KISS OR NOT TO KISS

"If a boy tried to kiss a girl of short acquaintance, she was indignant and whispered about it to the other girls the next day. According to our code, only engaged couples had the right to display affection, and even they should be reserved.

"That was 1914. Skip to 1924… Some of the crowd had adopted casual kissing as a matter of course, though it was still frowned upon. Girls with a reputation for indulging in 'petting parties' were not considered nice. It was unheard of to receive propositions from boys in one's own set, though some girls had thrilling tales of 'attempted seductions,' by men they'd met through work or while travelling… [By 1934] 'necking' was as casual and unblushing as handshaking with most of the crowd, and two minutes in a parked car or dark corner would take certain lads farther than my husband had ventured in a two-year engagement."

from "Flaming Youth Cool Off!" by Mrs. Rip Van Winkle, August 1935

FEBRUARY

MONDAY

21   Heritage Day
1990 kd lang wins the Grammy award for best female country vocalist

TUESDAY

22

WEDNESDAY

23   1944 Agnes MacPhail becomes the first woman sworn into the Ontario Legislature

THURSDAY

24   b.1972 Manon Rhéaume, first woman to play a Junior A men's hockey game

FRIDAY

25

SATURDAY ◑

26

SUNDAY

27

October 1928 issue

FEBRUARY

S	M	T	W	T	F	S
		1	2	3	4	5
6	7	8	9	10	11	12
13	14	15	16	17	18	19
20	21	22	23	24	25	26
27	28	29				

1920s HIPPIES?

Tie-dying wasn't invented by hippies in the 1960s, it was actually a fad from the late 1920s. *Chatelaine* recommended tie-dying as a technique for decorating curtains, cushions, bedspreads, runners, lampshades, hand-bags, kimonos and even "fancy-dress costumes."

CHATELAINE

MARCH 1938 · TEN CENTS

Chapeaux

			MARCH			
S	M	T	W	T	F	S
				1	2	3	4
5	6	7	8	9	10	11
12	13	14	15	16	17	18
19	20	21	22	23	24	25
26	27	28	29	30	31	

FEBRUARY/MARCH

MONDAY

28

TUESDAY

29

WEDNESDAY

1
1971 Eight women are jailed for protesting the All-Male Jury Law

THURSDAY

2
d.1945 Emily Carr, painter and author

FRIDAY

3
d.1962 Cairine Reay Wilson, first woman appointed to the Canadian Senate

SATURDAY

4

SUNDAY

5

MARCH

MONDAY ●

6

TUESDAY

7   d.1913 Pauline Johnson, poet, writer and Chautauqua performer

WEDNESDAY

8
Ash Wednesday
International Women's Day
b.1896 Charlotte Whitton, first woman elected mayor of Ottawa

THURSDAY

9   1883 The Toronto Women's Literary Society disbands and reorganizes as the Toronto Women's Suffrage Association

FRIDAY

10 b.1796 Julia Catherine Hart, author

SATURDAY

11

SUNDAY

12

Clara Brett Martin, Ontario's first woman barrister, August 1929 issue

MARCH

S	M	T	W	T	F	S
			1	2	3	4
5	6	7	8	9	10	11
12	13	14	15	16	17	18
19	20	21	22	23	24	25
26	27	28	29	30	31	

WOMEN AND THE LAW

Although women have been permitted to practise law in Ontario since 1897, only about sixty-seven have graduated, and of these only fifteen or sixteen are actually practising. Women struggled long and hard to gain admittance to the bar, but it was not until after the war, when a general change in the status and outlook of women took place, that they took to the trail that Clara Brett Martin had blazed, in any great numbers. Miss Vera L. Parsons is of the opinion that law is not as yet a popular profession among women themselves, and for the scarcity of women practising it, lays the blame to a large extent at the door of matrimony. It is generally true, she says, that of four women who graduate, two will begin to practise law, one will marry and one will take a position in which her legal training is an advantage; then a little later one of the two practising law will marry.

from "Women in the World," April 1929

Women's Health and Healing

Augusta Stowe Gullen was the first woman to graduate from medical school in Canada. She followed in the footsteps of her mother, Emily Stowe, the first woman to practise medicine in Canada.

Mary Agnes Snively, also known as the Florence Nightingale of Canada, laid the foundation for nursing in this country. She fought, and won, the right for nurses to have scientific training, something which was largely considered a "frill" in the nineteenth century. Not only a nurse, Snively was a talented administrator, diplomat and organizer.

HYGIENIC FIXATIONS OF THE 1930s

Personal Daintiness
(posture and neatness)

Regularity

Feminine Hygiene

Feminine Odour
(of a personal nature)

Under-arm Odour

Pink Toothbrush (bleeding gums)

"Domestic" Hands (wrinkled hands)

Bad Breath

SHE WANTS TO KNOW BUT SHE HATES TO ASK

Women were instrumental in establishing Canada's health care system, and took most of the responsibility for the health of their families. Their own concerns, however, were rarely mentioned and often cloaked in secrecy. Advertisements for products from companies like Lysol and Zonite warned about the potential dangers of neglecting feminine hygiene—dangers that ranged from a variety of unnamed illnesses to even the loss of a husband's love.

Early advertisements in *Chatelaine* reveal a society that was increasingly concerned with feminine odour. While Victorian beauty regimens recommended bathing every few weeks, by the 1920s women were warned that bathing even once a day wasn't enough to stave off the potential "horrible" problem of odour. Deodorant became one of the most popular items for women and men. Odour could ruin a potential relationship, a marriage, a possible job opportunity and even a friendship.

January 1943 issue

By the 1920s nutrition was a science. Vitamins C and D had been isolated and *Chatelaine* began to urge its readers to take a scientific approach to planning meals for their families.

MARCH

MONDAY ◑

13

TUESDAY

14 b.1868 Emily Murphy, first woman magistrate and appellant in the "Persons" case

WEDNESDAY

15

THURSDAY

16

FRIDAY

17 St. Patrick's Day

SATURDAY

18 b.1895 Grace MacLennan Grant Campbell, author

SUNDAY ○

19 d.1947 Prudence Heward, painter

October 1928 issue

THE LINE OF BEAUTY

All you have to do is go shopping for dresses to realize that corsets are a "must" this season. Without them your frocks and your figure are apt to disagree about points of interest, and you may look pretty disjointed. Everybody talks about the scissors silhouette, the hourglass figure, the wasp waist; the "corseted" look. This year your foundation is as much a part of your costume as your shoes and stockings, only more so.

from "Behind That Corseted Look," October 1939

MARCH

S	M	T	W	T	F	S
				1	2	3	4
5	6	7	8	9	10	11
12	13	14	15	16	17	18
19	20	21	22	23	24	25
26	27	28	29	30	31	

MARCH

MONDAY

20
Vernal Equinox

TUESDAY

21
b.1905 Phyllis McGinley, Canadian-born winner of the 1961 Pulitzer prize for poetry

WEDNESDAY

22
b.1909 Gabrielle Roy, author

THURSDAY

23

FRIDAY

24
b.1890 Agnes MacPhail, first woman MPP

SATURDAY

25

SUNDAY

26

Northern Electric advertisement, November 1946 issue

MARCH

S	M	T	W	T	F	S
				1	2	3	4
5	6	7	8	9	10	11
12	13	14	15	16	17	18
19	20	21	22	23	24	25
26	27	28	29	30	31	

A DIPLOMATIC HUSBAND

I let my wife spoil me—because she likes it. As all women, she likes to feel that she's a martyr to a cause. I'm the "cause" and she is never so happy as when she thinks I am imposing on her good nature and generosity. For instance, I don't care for breakfast. A cup of coffee completely suffices. I could easily get that cup of coffee on my way to the office and save a lot of trouble and probably get better coffee; but I don't. Promptly at seven-thirty, my good wife arouses herself, sets the table and, by the time I'm shaved and dressed, has my coffee ready and waiting. Personally, although I don't press the point, I think it's rather silly. There's no reason why she should get up, except that secretly I know—although she sometimes grumbles about it—she enjoys the feeling of self-sacrifice it gives her.

from "Why I Let My Wife Spoil Me" by A Diplomatic Husband, January 1932

March/April

MONDAY ◑

27

TUESDAY

28 b.1951 Karen Kain, ballet dancer

WEDNESDAY

29

THURSDAY

30

FRIDAY

31

SATURDAY

1 1990 Carol Anne Letheren becomes the first woman president of the Canadian Olympic Association

SUNDAY

2 Daylight saving time begins

YOU'VE COME
THE WRONG WAY…BABY

Women were not yet "persons" under the law in 1928, but savvy advertisers didn't ignore their economic power. For years, only the most fatale of femmes smoked a cigarette, let alone a cigar, but this ad for United Cigar Stores insisted cigars were, indeed, "For Ladies Too!" Society's disapproval of women who smoked allowed advertisers to jump on the women's emancipation bandwagon to advertise their products, and there was a dramatic rise in the number of female smokers. As one *Chatelaine* writer put it, "It was more or less a badge of modernity. If a girl refused cigarettes, she explained it was because of her bronchial trouble or her singing lessons."

CHATELAINE

APRIL, 1939 ○ TEN CENTS

In This Issue:
A Complete Nov
*"Lightning Can
Strike Twice"*
By Elizabeth York Mil

FEATURING THE SPRING FASHION STORY

			APRIL			
S	M	T	W	T	F	S
						1
2	3	4	5	6	7	8
9	10	11	12	13	14	15
16	17	18	19	20	21	22
23	24	25	26	27	28	29
30						

APRIL

MONDAY

3
b.1876 Margaret Anglin, stage actress

TUESDAY ●

4

WEDNESDAY

5

THURSDAY

6

FRIDAY

7

SATURDAY

8
d.1885 Susanna Moodie, author

SUNDAY

9
b.1893 Mary Pickford, Canadian-born film star

APRIL

MONDAY

10 1974 Pauline McGibbon, first woman lieutenant-governor of Ontario

TUESDAY ◑

11 b.1922 Mavis Gallant, author

WEDNESDAY

12

THURSDAY

13

FRIDAY

14 1980 Jeanne Sauvé becomes the first woman Speaker of the House of Commons

SATURDAY

15 d.1964 Alice Evelyn Wilson, geologist and first woman to be admitted to the Fellowship of the Royal Society of Canada

SUNDAY

16

Helen Gregory MacGill, judge of the Juvenile Court, Vancouver, B.C., July 1929 issue

A WOMAN'S LIFE

It is obvious that more women are not involved with public life for three reasons: First, lack of confidence. Second, lack of funds. Third, lack of understanding that suffrage is a means and not an end. This attitude is perhaps reinforced by the fact that political parties work feverishly to offer women as many glittering generalities or positions of honor, without salaries, as possible. It has taken a few years to learn once more that all that glitters is not gold.

from "Are Women Wanted in Public Life?" by Helen Gregory MacGill, MA, September 1928

APRIL

S	M	T	W	T	F	S
						1
2	3	4	5	6	7	8
9	10	11	12	13	14	15
16	17	18	19	20	21	22
23	24	25	26	27	28	29
30						

CAREER GIRLS

During the 1920s and 1930s occupations for women were limited: women who worked tended to be either domestics, stenographers, secretaries, teachers or nurses. However, more and more women were graduating from university, some with professional degrees, though they were expected to devote themselves, full-time, to the task of being a wife and mother upon marriage. In some cases, they weren't given any choice.

"Most people believe that married women enter business life for one of three reasons. To have extra 'pin money' to live luxuriously on a double income; or to escape the monotony of housework. Cheered on by the populace, the University of Toronto decided to dismiss all married women on their staff, except those who were the sole support of their families, wives of disabled veterans, or special experts. When the reckoning came, out of the hundreds of women on the staff, just ten were affected."

from "Women in the World, A Page of Comment on Topics and Events,"
March 1932

In 1935 there were 14,368 Canadian women working as "hello girls"—that is, taking telephone orders for retail companies. Many of these women were the sole support of their families or worked to supplement the household income after their husbands suffered pay cuts or lost their jobs.

"I do a man's job. But the Boss told me that the reason they do not pay girls as much as men is because a girl will probably go off and get married just as soon as she is properly trained and getting useful. I ventured to remark that when a boy is well-trained some other firm grabs him, but he just shot me an uncomprehending stare and grunted caustically, 'It's different with men.'"

from "I Would Rather Have Beauty than Brains" by Nan Robins, 1931

During the Second World War, many employers went from banning women employees to an 8 percent female payroll. And many discovered that the women were actually better at the work than the men.

Telephone operator,
November 1932 issue

February 1943 issue

APRIL

MONDAY

17 1919 Women in New Brunswick win the right to vote in provincial elections

TUESDAY ○

18 b.1914 Claire Faucher, French-Canadian author and winner of the Prix du Cercle du Livre du France

WEDNESDAY

19 1916 Women in Alberta win the right to vote and hold political office

THURSDAY

20 First day of Passover

FRIDAY

21 Good Friday

SATURDAY

22 Earth Day

SUNDAY

23 Easter Sunday
Canada Book Day
b.1918 Margaret Avison, poet

APRIL

S	M	T	W	T	F	S
						1
2	3	4	5	6	7	8
9	10	11	12	13	14	15
16	17	18	19	20	21	22
23	24	25	26	27	28	29
30						

THE ORIGIN OF ANNE WITH AN E

People ask me how I came to create Anne. I didn't create her. She simply sprang into being in my mind, already created—Anne, spelled with an e, red-haired, dreamy-eyed and elfin-faced. Yet she seemed so real to me that when I tell people she is "entirely fictitious" I have the uncomfortable feeling I am not telling the truth. People ask me, too, why I gave her red hair. I didn't. It *was* red. And as I described her long red braids as she sat on the shingle pile at Bright River Station, I didn't foresee a curious situation in the future when four prominent lawyers of the Boston Bar would sit around a table piled high with dictionaries and books of engravings, and argue heatedly for three mortal days over the exact tint of Anne's tresses. Were they or were they not Titian red? And if they were, then just what shade exactly was Titian red?

from "Is This My Anne?" by Lucy Maud Montgomery, January 1935

WHAT EVERY MOTHER SHOULD KNOW

For many women, particularly those who lived in remote and isolated areas of Canada, *Chatelaine* was often the only, if not the most readily available source of medical and child-rearing advice. In the 1920s, 30s and 40s, *Chatelaine* featured an advice column for new mothers entitled "*Chatelaine*'s Baby Clinic." Women were encouraged to write in with their questions and concerns, and these were addressed by a professional medical doctor hired by *Chatelaine* and also, whenever possible, with *Chatelaine*'s helpful family guide for new mothers entitled *The Baby Book*. This book provided detailed information about child-care and recommended products which had been subjected to extensive testing in the laboratories of the *Chatelaine* Institute.

This open forum for mothers was often an invaluable source of information for many new mothers. Many of the problems were easily rectified, as in the case of one Saskatchewan mother who wrote to the "Baby Clinic" in 1935:

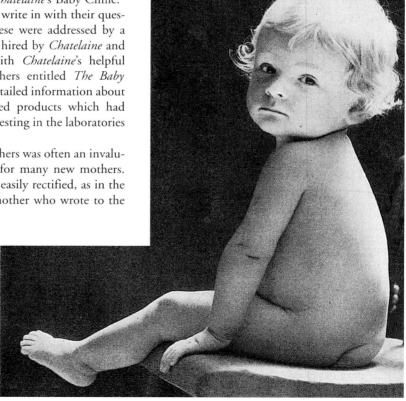

Tested and Approved by
SERIAL 0—— NO. 00
The **Chatelaine Institute**
MAINTAINED BY
The Chatelaine Magazine

QUESTION : My daughter, four months old, weighs sixteen pounds. She is fed every three hours and vomits a good deal and has hiccoughs. She is restless at night. Please send Baby Book.

RESPONSE: Your girl is about three pounds above the average weight. The symptoms you mention indicate overfeeding. Try feeding at 3 ½ to four hours and check up your formula with that of the Baby Book sent.

APRIL

MONDAY

24 d.1942 Lucy Maud Montgomery, author of *Anne of Green Gables*

TUESDAY

25 1940 Quebec grants women the right to vote

WEDNESDAY ◑

26 b.1922 Jeanne Sauvé, first woman governor-general

THURSDAY

27

FRIDAY

28

SATURDAY

29

SUNDAY

30

October 1939 issue

THE PERFECT DIONNES

In 1934 the birth of the Dionne Quints was heralded as a miracle of modern medical science. Emilie, Cécile, Marie, Yvonne and Annette became an overnight marketing sensation. Their faces were used to promote everything from spoons to soup to soap. They were billed as the "perfect children." Even their home was a perfect miniature, scientifically measured and adjusted to fit the Quints during their growing years. Each day their routine was precisely worked out by an expert in preschool training and a specialist in child psychology. At ten o'clock each day, hats and coats went on for outside play in the "observation yard," where, even in the winter, hundreds of tourists from all over North America would come in busloads to observe the Dionnes at play.

APRIL

S	M	T	W	T	F	S
						1
2	3	4	5	6	7	8
9	10	11	12	13	14	15
16	17	18	19	20	21	22
23	24	25	26	27	28	29
30						

CHATELAINE

Ten Cents
MAY 1941

Featuring
The 1941 BRIDE

			MAY			
S	M	T	W	T	F	S
			1	2	3	4	5	6
7	8	9	10	11	12	13
14	15	16	17	18	19	20
21	22	23	24	25	26	27
28	29	30	31			

MAY

MONDAY

1   b.1831 Dr. Emily Stowe, suffragist and first woman to practise medicine in Canada

TUESDAY

2

WEDNESDAY

3   b.1933 Mary Ellen Smith, MLA, first woman cabinet minister in the British Empire

THURSDAY ●

4

FRIDAY

5   b.1923 Cathleen Morawetz, Canadian mathematician, and the first woman to head an American mathematics institute

SATURDAY

6

SUNDAY

7

MAY

MONDAY

8

TUESDAY

9

WEDNESDAY ◑

10 b.1929 Antonine Maillet, first Canadian to win the Prix Goncourt, France's most prestigious literary prize

THURSDAY

11

FRIDAY

12

SATURDAY

13

SUNDAY

14 Mother's Day

Elizabeth Arden, circa 1928

MAY

S	M	T	W	T	F	S
	1	2	3	4	5	6
7	8	9	10	11	12	13
14	15	16	17	18	19	20
21	22	23	24	25	26	27
28	29	30	31			

EVERY WOMAN HAS A RIGHT TO BE BEAUTIFUL

She said, "Every woman has a right to be beautiful" and built a multimillion-dollar empire showing them how. A self-made millionaire, Elizabeth Arden's success story was well known in her day, though very few knew that she was from Woodbridge, Ontario. Born in the late nineteenth century as Florence Nightingale Graham, she began her career as a nurse. At that time, only a "fallen" woman would "paint" her face. When she changed her own name to Elizabeth Arden, she also set out to give cosmetics a better one.

She started with a sumptuously decorated salon and a simple moisturizer and by the 1940s her line of beauty products had become a multimillion-dollar business. Her Fifth Avenue salon served the cream of New York society and the Elizabeth Arden chain was one of the most prestigious in America.

Until her death at the age of eighty-one, Arden maintained complete control over her company. She owned all of the stock and she acted as president and chairman of the board of every Elizabeth Arden company in the world.

May

MONDAY

15

TUESDAY

16 d.1915 "Kit" Coleman, the world's first woman war correspondent

WEDNESDAY

17

THURSDAY ○

18

FRIDAY

19

SATURDAY

20 1986 Canadian mountaineer Sharon Wood becomes the first North American woman to reach the summit of Mount Everest

SUNDAY

21

A VERSE FOR A FLOWER VASE SHOWER

There's nothing that changes a dwelling so much
As that which is known as the feminine touch
And nothing more kin to the feminine soul
Than just the right flowers in just the right bowl!

from "The Successful Shower Hostess," June 1932

June 1929 issue

MAY

S	M	T	W	T	F	S
	1	2	3	4	5	6
7	8	9	10	11	12	13
14	15	16	17	18	19	20
21	22	23	24	25	26	27
28	29	30	31			

May

MONDAY		
22	Victoria Day 1979 Ten women are elected to the House of Commons, the most to that date	
TUESDAY		
23		
WEDNESDAY		
24	1918 Women win the right to vote in federal elections and hold federal office	
THURSDAY		
25		
FRIDAY ◑		
26	b.1899 Muriel McQueen Fergusson, first woman Speaker of the Senate	
SATURDAY		
27		
SUNDAY		
28	b.1934 Dionne quintuplets	

June 1943 issue

THE GREAT DEBATE OVER...PANTS

"Women weren't made to wear trousers. Designed for men, nothing looks worse on most women than designed-for-men pants." "They make you look big." "They do, after all, present you more or less as you really are. So if you must wear 'em, be sure to wear a very good panty-girdle and a good brassiere is more important than ever." The debate over women wearing pants was a lengthy one and the loudest opposition came from the men. However, once women were more or less forced into trousers with their entry to the workplace, it was impossible to get them out of them. In the end *Chatelaine* acquiesced, saying, "Well, if you *must* wear 'em..."

from "Should Women Wear Pants?" June 1943

MAY						
S	M	T	W	T	F	S
	1	2	3	4	5	6
7	8	9	10	11	12	13
14	15	16	17	18	19	20
21	22	23	24	25	26	27
28	29	30	31			

Chatelaine

JUNE, 1946
TEN CENTS

The Canadian Woman's Magazine

JUNE

S	M	T	W	T	F	S
				1	2	3
4	5	6	7	8	9	10
11	12	13	14	15	16	17
18	19	20	21	22	23	24
25	26	27	28	29	30	

May/June

MONDAY	
29	b.1894 Bea Lillie, comedienne
TUESDAY	
30	
WEDNESDAY	
31	d.1963 Grace MacLennan Grant Campbell, author
THURSDAY	
1	
FRIDAY ●	
2	
SATURDAY	
3	
SUNDAY	
4	

JUNE

MONDAY

5
d.1966 Dorothy Stevens, artist

TUESDAY

6

WEDNESDAY

7
1917 Louise McKinney and Roberta MacAdams of Alberta become the first women elected to a provincial legislature

THURSDAY ◑

8

FRIDAY

9
1982 Bertha Wilson becomes the first woman appointed to the Supreme Court

SATURDAY

10
d.1979 Kay McIver, one of the CBC's first woman radio producers

SUNDAY

11

May 1932 issue

WHO WAS MAZO DE LA ROCHE?

When *Jalna* won *The Atlantic Monthly*'s $10,000 prize for fiction in 1927, Mazo de la Roche shot to world-wide fame almost overnight. *Jalna* then grew into a sixteen-novel saga, detailing the lives of a large family living on a large Ontario estate. An enigmatic figure in Canadian letters, Mazo de la Roche was intensely secretive about her personal life. The biographical information she did give out was often wildly conflicting. When her novel *The Thunder of New Wings* appeared as a serial in *Chatelaine,* then editor Byrne Hope Sanders wrote a glowing profile to announce it. In a recent biography, however, Joan Givner proves the details Miss de la Roche provided about her French Royalist heritage, her early childhood, even her place of birth and the names of her adopted children were a complete fabrication.

JUNE

S	M	T	W	T	F	S
				1	2	3
4	5	6	7	8	9	10
11	12	13	14	15	16	17
18	19	20	21	22	23	24
25	26	27	28	29	30	

Canadian Girls Hit the Silver Screen

Alexis Smith

Norma Shearer as Marie Antoinette

Hollywood films and starlets were an important part of the social fabric for Canadians throughout the twentieth century, particularly when the war interfered with day-to-day activities. Films were often an excellent way of delaying reality for a few hours. *Chatelaine* often featured various Hollywood starlets between its covers. The glamour of Hollywood offered the thrill of mystery and romance to women who stayed at home to take care of their families, and the glamour associated with Hollywood was an easily adaptable and accessible marketing tool for a wide variety of products.

Hollywood glamour girls were a particular favourite. In the 1930s, 40s and 50s, when women were constantly being reminded of the importance of looking their best (never letting their noses shine), film starlets were commonly used to advocate a variety of different beauty products, from deodorant to nail lacquer. Judy Garland blithely advocated deodorant, Joan Crawford touted matte face powder, and Veronica Lake confessed to an addiction to Ruby Red lipstick. Style was a hot commodity, and Hollywood glamour girls had style in spades.

Whenever possible Canadian stars were also featured in the pages of *Chatelaine.* Mary Pickford was, of course, Canada's sweetheart as well as Hollywood's; Marie Dressler was acclaimed for her Academy Award and Norma Shearer revered for her beauty. They, too, revealed their beauty secrets to fans at home.

Mary Pickford

Yvonne DeCarlo

Mary Pickford

Mary Pickford was a significant star in the early years of Hollywood. She was one of the first stars of the silent film era to make the transition to talking pictures. With her beautiful, long, blond ringlets and sweet smile, she became so popular she was dubbed "America's Sweetheart," but she was born right here in Canada.

Alexis Smith

Born in Penticton, B.C., Alexis Smith was spotted by a talent scout as she played the lead in amateur theatricals put on by her fellow college students. The screen test that followed proved so successful that she was given the feminine lead opposite Errol Flynn in *Dive Bomber*—a flying start that won her a place right up in the rarefied atmosphere of stardom.

Norma Shearer

In 1938 Canadian-born Norma Shearer played the ultimate glamour girl in Hollywood's production of *Marie Antoinette*.

Beatrice Lillie

Bea Lillie was one of the most popular stars of England's stage and screen in the early part of the century. One journalist wrote that she was "quite simply, the funniest woman in the world." Few of her fans knew, however, that she was born in Toronto, at the corner of Queen and Dovercourt.

Yvonne DeCarlo

Yvonne DeCarlo was one of Vancouver's very first gifts to Hollywood when she won a beauty contest that gave her small roles in a number of Hollywood films.

Beatrice Lillie

June

MONDAY

12 d.1961 Mazo de la Roche, author

TUESDAY

13

WEDNESDAY

14

THURSDAY

15

FRIDAY ○

16 1880 Dr. Emily Stowe becomes the first woman member of the Physicians and Surgeons of Ontario

SATURDAY

17

SUNDAY

18 Father's Day

June 1928 issue

S	M	T	W	T	F	S
				1	2	3
4	5	6	7	8	9	10
11	12	13	14	15	16	17
18	19	20	21	22	23	24
25	26	27	28	29	30	

THE BRIDE'S HOPE CHEST, AND THINGS TO GO IN IT

The prosperous years between the First World War and the Depression allowed women to enjoy the luxury of hope and dreams of future romance. One feature of this renewed optimism was the resurging popularity of the hope chest. Only the most charming collection of household items were invited into its sacred domain: hand-embroidered blankets, finest quality linen bedspreads, appliqué dinner cloths, silver luncheon sets and appliqué towels. These treasures were collected over the years and carefully laid away in a cedar chest until the woman's wedding day.

JUNE

MONDAY

19

TUESDAY

20

WEDNESDAY

21 1957 Ellen Fairclough is appointed Secretary of State, becoming the first woman federal cabinet minister

THURSDAY

22

FRIDAY

23

SATURDAY ◑

24 Saint-Jean-Baptiste Day
1909 International Congress of Women opens in Toronto

SUNDAY

25 1993 Kim Campbell becomes Canada's first woman prime minister

June 1934 issue

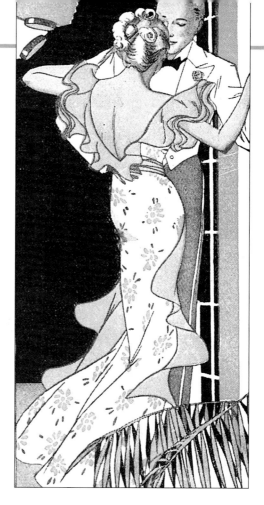

MARRY NOW?

Oh yes! Take the chance. We did it. Before we married, my husband and I both occupied good positions. We had planned marriage for two years but along came the panic and we were both let out, so my "to be" husband said: "We may as well 'swim' as sink"; and disregarding advice from world-wise mothers and reluctant dads—we took the plunge into the matrimonial sea.

After futile attempts to secure employment through the medium of the press, the primal urge which brought our forebears over the rolling ocean to seek their destiny in a new world, asserted itself and we decided to go to the wide spaces and secure a homestead.

from "Marry Now? Yes" Eureka, April 1934

JUNE

S	M	T	W	T	F	S
				1	2	3
4	5	6	7	8	9	10
11	12	13	14	15	16	17
18	19	20	21	22	23	24
25	26	27	28	29	30	

JUNE/JULY

MONDAY

26

TUESDAY

27

WEDNESDAY

28

THURSDAY

29

FRIDAY

30

SATURDAY ●

1
Canada Day
1916 Emily Murphy and Alice Jamieson become the first women in the British Empire to be appointed police magistrates

SUNDAY

2

April 1939 issue

She's a Nice Girl, but . . .

Susie dangles with her pumps till all the young men get the jumps.

And Geraldine the Girdle-Twister wonders why romance has mis't her . . .

Mary slaps the powder on and says: "Where HAS that nice boy gone . . ."

And Hattie's hope chest is QUITE bare —she's always fussing with her hair . . .

They like the girl who straightens seams . . . but NOT in thoroughfares, it seems . .

Alas! The world was Mary's oyster till she became a slip-strap hoister.

And Bernadette, who plays with beads, has lost that LOVELY male in tweeds . . .

Need one remark—the gurgle-lassie is very passé.

Thumbs down on constant lip-retraces . . . and oh! the woman who pulls faces!

If habits such as these you own, don't wonder why you live alone.

JULY

S M T W T F S

1

2 3 4 5 6 7 8

9 10 11 12 13 14 15

16 17 18 19 20 21 22

23 24 25 26 27 28 29

30 31

CHATELAINE

Ten Cents

JULY 1941

JULY						
S	M	T	W	T	F	S
						1
2	3	4	5	6	7	8
9	10	11	12	13	14	15
16	17	18	19	20	21	22
23	24	25	26	27	28	29
30	31					

JULY

MONDAY

3

TUESDAY

4
American Independence Day

WEDNESDAY

5

THURSDAY

6

FRIDAY

7

SATURDAY

8

SUNDAY

9

July

MONDAY

10   b.1931 Alice Munro, author

TUESDAY

11

WEDNESDAY

12

THURSDAY

13   1908 Women compete in the Olympic Games for the first time

FRIDAY

14

SATURDAY

15   d.1958 Dr. Marion Hilliard, physician and author

SUNDAY ○

16

September 1928 issue

NORA-FRANCES HENDERSON

Nora-Frances Henderson's first ambition was to become a boy. She succeeded in becoming Canada's first woman municipal controller. She began her career as a columnist for the *Hamilton Herald,* writing the gossip column "Mrs. Peep's Diary" and another on current affairs slugged "In Feminine Focus." In 1929, she began using her column to urge women to sit on the Hospital Board, and was chiefly responsible for the Board's nomination of four women. She then began to encourage women to run for municipal office, and a group of women offered to nominate her. She was elected in 1931, and sat for sixteen consecutive terms in Hamilton city government.

JULY

S	M	T	W	T	F	S
						1
2	3	4	5	6	7	8
9	10	11	12	13	14	15
16	17	18	19	20	21	22
23	24	25	26	27	28	29
30	31					

JULY

MONDAY

17

TUESDAY

18   b.1926 Margaret Laurence, author

WEDNESDAY

19

THURSDAY

20

FRIDAY

21

SATURDAY

22

SUNDAY

23

March 1941 issue

HOME DISCOVERIES

To Prevent Burning Cakes

When baking a fruit cake which requires to be in the oven a long time, sprinkle a layer of corn meal in your pan before lining it with buttered paper. If your oven should be too hot, the cornmeal will take the scorch and the cake will be safe from burnt bottoms.

—*M.M., Port Elgin, Ontario, 1931*

JULY

S	M	T	W	T	F	S
						1
2	3	4	5	6	7	8
9	10	11	12	13	14	15
16	17	18	19	20	21	22
23	24	25	26	27	28	29
30	31					

July

MONDAY ◑

24

TUESDAY

25 b.1923 Cathleen Callbeck, the first woman to be elected premier of P.E.I. and the first woman premier in Canada

WEDNESDAY

26

THURSDAY

27

FRIDAY

28

SATURDAY

29

SUNDAY ●

30

June 1946 issue

JULY

S	M	T	W	T	F	S
						1
2	3	4	5	6	7	8
9	10	11	12	13	14	15
16	17	18	19	20	21	22
23	24	25	26	27	28	29
30	31					

BIKINIS MAKE A BIG SPLASH

The news in bathing suits, whether we like it or not, is nudity! It's a discreet nudity suggested by adroit form-fitting lines that give sun-eager skins more than a peek at the great big world!

from "Water Babies," June 1946

CHATELAINE

Ten Cents

AUGUST 1941

AUGUST

S	M	T	W	T	F	S
				1	2	3	4	5
6	7	8	9	10	11	12
13	14	15	16	17	18	19
20	21	22	23	24	25	26
27	28	29	30	31		

July/August

MONDAY	
31	1928 Alys McKey Bryant takes off from Vancouver, becoming the first Canadian woman to pilot an airplane
TUESDAY	
1	b.1905 Helen Battles Hogg-Priestley, first Canadian to win the Klumpke-Roberts Award, for her contribution to the public's understanding of astronomy
WEDNESDAY	
2	b.1780 Marie-Anne Lagemodière, first French-Canadian woman in the Canadian West
THURSDAY	
3	
FRIDAY	
4	
SATURDAY	
5	
SUNDAY ◐	
6	

August

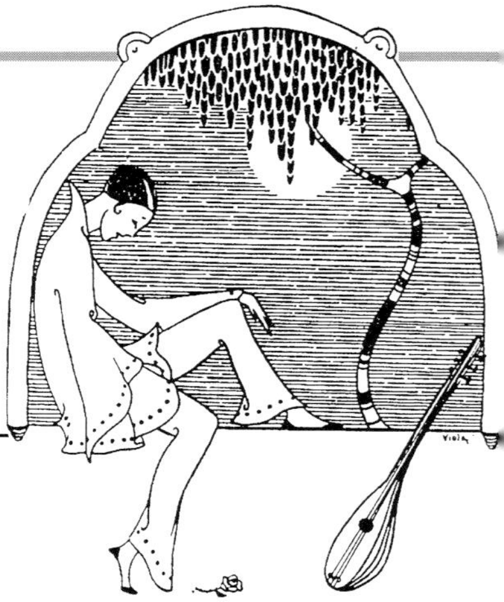

MONDAY

7   Civic Holiday

TUESDAY

8

WEDNESDAY

9

THURSDAY

10

FRIDAY

11

SATURDAY

12

SUNDAY

13

March 1928 issue

GERTRUDE HUNTLY

In the early part of the century, Gertrude Huntly was one of Canada's most distinguished classical musicians. A brilliant pianist as well as a gifted violinist, she began her musical career as a student at the Music Conservatory in London, Ontario. At only twelve-years-old, she won the Barron gold medal and the Heintzman scholarship, the school's highest honours. The Conservatory's director advised her parents to send her abroad, so at sixteen, she went to Paris. She quickly attracted the attention of the most respected musicians of the day, pianist and composer Maurice Moszkowsky and Albert Geloso, a master violinist. She was still in her teens when she made her Paris debut assisted by both distinguished masters.

AUGUST						
S	M	T	W	T	F	S
			1	2	3	4	5
6	7	8	9	10	11	12
13	14	15	16	17	18	19
20	21	22	23	24	25	26
27	28	29	30	31		

The Women's Club Movement

During the late nineteenth century, women began forming small clubs aimed at improving various conditions within their communities. By the 1930s the Women's Institute was a firmly established national society, and all across Canada women were at work building hospitals and orphanages, improving school systems, planting trees, distributing garden seeds and helping with the sick and destitute.

Chatelaine profiled many of these ordinary Canadians in the regular feature "Women and their Work." Though these women were acting locally, they were thinking globally, working for peace and improved conditions the world over, through the organization of the International Council of Women.

Mrs. H.M. Hilliker

"Twenty-four years ago Mrs. Hilliker, with her little boy of three and a five-months-old baby, followed her husband into the West. For some years she lived, first at Viking and then at Minburn, Alberta, where there was no doctor within twenty-five miles. Many were the people she helped with her knowledge of nursing and her readiness at all times to be of assistance. When the railway came to Viking and with it a doctor and a good school, the Hillikers moved

back. During the war, she took an active part in Red Cross work, and since then she worked very hard with the Women's Institute to establish the Viking Municipal Hospital."

from "Women and their Work," April 1932

"The vision presented of women from all parts of the world meeting together and rising above all political, religious and racial differences, to concentrate every effort of mind and spirit in a mass drive towards peace, was one to inspire hope." —Winnifred Kydd

While still in her twenties, Winnifred Kydd became the president of the National Council of Women. She was the only woman full-time delegate from the British Empire at the 1932 Disarmament Conference in Geneva. She also represented Canadian women at the International Council of Women in the summer of 1934.

Winnifred Kydd, president of the National Council of Women

Adelaide Plumptre, Canadian delegate to the League of Nations

Mary Agnes Snively, one of our greatest Canadian women, who laid the foundation for Canadian nursing

AUGUST

MONDAY

14

TUESDAY ○

15

WEDNESDAY

16

THURSDAY

17

FRIDAY

18

SATURDAY

19 d.1963 Kathleen Parlow, violinist

SUNDAY

20

January 1929 issue

DRIVING THE AUTO INDUSTRY

Auto-makers have long been aware that women are a driving force in the new car market. Ford, Chrysler and GM all advertised in *Chatelaine* from the very beginning, with images of fashionable women behind the wheel. They knew that women had a say in major family purchases and—as "The New Woman" became active in her community and the world of work—more were actually driving. Manufacturers began to design vehicles, as one advertisement put it, "with feminine tastes in mind." Cars were becoming safer, quieter and more comfortable. A car's appearance—inside and out—became increasingly important. Women demanded luxurious plush interiors, slick body design in a range of colours and attractive details, and auto-makers were quick to comply.

AUGUST

S	M	T	W	T	F	S
		1	2	3	4	5
6	7	8	9	10	11	12
13	14	15	16	17	18	19
20	21	22	23	24	25	26
27	28	29	30	31		

August

MONDAY

21 d.1968 Germaine Guèvremont, author of the Governor-General's Award-winning novel *The Outlander*

TUESDAY ◐

22

WEDNESDAY

23

THURSDAY

24

FRIDAY

25

SATURDAY

26

SUNDAY

27

NYLON ON THE HOME FRONT!

Nylon is back from the war! Back from the four corners of the world, back from the European skies and the southern Pacific atolls comes the fabric of the future! It was nylon, you remember, that soared through the clouds in the form of parachutes, sailed the high seas in life-saving dinghies, brought comfortable sleeping hammocks to war-weary fighting men…filtered blood plasma…saved lives in surgical sutures.

Nylon has returned to civilian life, and, entering a happier service, now leads the parade of the breath-taking new fabrics of peacetime fashions.

from "First Fabric of the Future," February 1946

September 1946 issue

AUGUST

S	M	T	W	T	F	S
		1	2	3	4	5
6	7	8	9	10	11	12
13	14	15	16	17	18	19
20	21	22	23	24	25	26
27	28	29	30	31		

August/September

MONDAY

28

TUESDAY ●

29 d.1899 Catharine Parr Traill, author

WEDNESDAY

30

THURSDAY

31

FRIDAY

1 b.1941 Gwendolyn MacEwen, poet and novelist
d.1951 Nellie McClung, author, feminist and Alberta MLA 1921–1926

SATURDAY

2 d.1940 Maude Abbott, physician and educationist

SUNDAY

3

SEPTEMBER

S	M	T	W	T	F	S
					1	2
3	4	5	6	7	8	9
10	11	12	13	14	15	16
17	18	19	20	21	22	23
24	25	26	27	28	29	30

THE MODERNIST MOVEMENT

We have been privileged in the twentieth century to see the practical application of a new creative principle, modernism. Strange and often bizarre beyond our understanding, it has often seemed, yet fascinating; and when we have learned to accustom our minds and eyes to the rhythm of cycles, the harmony of planes, the huge design and contrast, even the sharp punctuation of angles, we have been able to see interest, if not beauty in its form and colour.

"The designer of today has shaken off the tyranny of curves, twists, twiddles and the confusing flow of ornamental line," writes John Cloag, the noted furniture historian, and he voices the basic characteristics of the new furniture age.

from "What Is This Modernist Movement?" by Anne Elizabeth Wilson, March 1928

Chatelaine

SEPTEMBER
Ten Cents

In This Issue:
Kay Murphy...on
Autumn Fashions

		SEPTEMBER				
S	M	T	W	T	F	S
					1	2
3	4	5	6	7	8	9
10	11	12	13	14	15	16
17	18	19	20	21	22	23
24	25	26	27	28	29	30

September

MONDAY

4 Labour Day

TUESDAY ☽

5

WEDNESDAY

6

THURSDAY

7

FRIDAY

8

SATURDAY

9

SUNDAY

10

September

MONDAY

11

TUESDAY

12

WEDNESDAY ○

13 b.1775 Laura Secord, heroine of the War of 1812

THURSDAY

14

FRIDAY

15

SATURDAY

16 b.1921 Ursula Franklin, first woman professor at the University of Toronto

SUNDAY

17

April 1938 issue

E. CORA HIND

In the early part of this century, E. Cora Hind was one of Canada's premier journalists. A world authority on agricultural affairs, when she began her career female reporters were virtually unheard of. Ms. Hind first broke into journalism writing for *The Free Press*. Her articles smashed Victorian conventions with their frank reports on livestock breeding problems. Hind had always been photographed in her trademark brown riding suit, but in 1938, *Chatelaine* managed to capture her in a more domestic pose—knitting by her fireplace in a silk dress.

SEPTEMBER

S	M	T	W	T	F	S
					1	2
3	4	5	6	7	8	9
10	11	12	13	14	15	16
17	18	19	20	21	22	23
24	25	26	27	28	29	30

For the Love of Fashion

Since the 1920s *Chatelaine* has been a guiding light on the fashion front. One of the first women's magazines to enter Canadian women's lives in the early part of the century, *Chatelaine* was eagerly awaited by many who lived in the far reaches of the Saskatchewan prairies or the isolated areas of eastern Nova Scotia. Often *Chatelaine* was the only source of popular fashion available to women who lived in these rural, isolated areas.

From their hats to their heels, *Chatelaine* has done its best to keep Canadian women up-to-date on changing styles and trends. When we went on our first big date we knew what to wear and how to wear it; when we went to our first job we wore the right lipstick and underwent the necessary home beauty remedy treatments to keep us fresh and "ready for when fate might walk through the door"; and when the men came home from the war we knew how to rival those femmes fatale from across the water, because *Chatelaine* was there all along, helping, showing and telling.

Hats were considered the height of fashion from the 1920s to the 1940s

If fashion demanded swirling lines and fluted cascades or rippling hemlines and windswept silhouettes, yellow for spring, black for sophistication and polka dots for fun, *Chatelaine* let the wise woman know, and showed her how to proceed if her budget couldn't measure up to all the finery. With pages in every early issue devoted to *Chatelaine* dress designs, women were able to create the latest fashion designs in their own homes.

Nighttime glamour from 1928

A business suit from the 1930s

September

MONDAY

18 b.1861 E. Cora Hind, journalist

TUESDAY

19 b.1915 Elizabeth Stern, Canadian-born cancer researcher

WEDNESDAY ☽

20 d.1965 Madge MacBeth, first woman president of the Canadian Authors Association

THURSDAY

21

FRIDAY

22 Autumnal Equinox

SATURDAY

23

SUNDAY

24

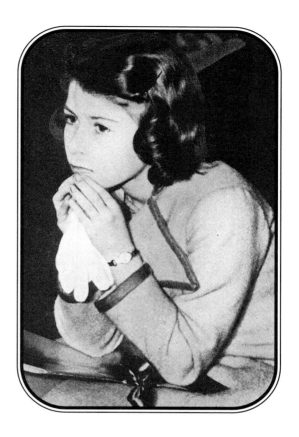

SEPTEMBER

S	M	T	W	T	F	S
					1	2
3	4	5	6	7	8	9
10	11	12	13	14	15	16
17	18	19	20	21	22	23
24	25	26	27	28	29	30

INTRODUCING THE PRINCESSES

During the 1930s, *Chatelaine* published numerous articles about the Princesses Elizabeth and Margaret Rose and their parents, the newly crowned King and Queen of England. One particularly intimate article by Lady Cynthia Asquith included informal photos taken by the King himself, and descriptions of the young Princesses' bedrooms. Fascination with the two little girls, who were once known as the "White Roses of York," created a market for all sorts of Royal memorabilia—including rag dolls in the image of Princess Elizabeth and Princess Margaret.

CHATELAINE

OCTOBER
1938
TEN CENTS

In This Issue: **Another Complete Novel** ... and **The Fall Fashions**

OCTOBER						
S	M	T	W	T	F	S
1	2	3	4	5	6	7
8	9	10	11	12	13	14
15	16	17	18	19	20	21
22	23	24	25	26	27	28
29	30	31				

September/October

MONDAY	
25	
TUESDAY	
26	
WEDNESDAY ●	
27	
THURSDAY	
28	
FRIDAY	
29	
SATURDAY	
30	Rosh Hashanah 1965 Laura Sabia of St. Catharines, Ontario, defends working women against charges of being "bad mothers" made by the Ontario Medical Association
SUNDAY	
1	

October

MONDAY

2

TUESDAY

3

d.1964 Maisie Hurley, founder and editor of the first First Nations newspaper *Native Voice*

WEDNESDAY

4

THURSDAY

5

FRIDAY

6

d.1942 E. Cora Hind, journalist

SATURDAY

7

SUNDAY

8

November 1946 issue

THOSE GOLDEN SLIPPERS...

Light as a flower petal...unbelievably flexible...they are the kind Salome's dancing feet would have loved! Hand-made, here and now, in Canada, by the Montreal designer, Del Grande, black suede and gold kid are alternated in flower design appliqués that bring new beauty to footwear fashions. Hinged trickery dividing the sole and heel gives freedom and comfort to feet that dance for hours and hours, and the very high platform adds inches to the wearer's height. An advance sign of the new season of glittering elegance and patiently perfected detail.

from "Chatelaine Fashions," September 1946

OCTOBER

S	M	T	W	T	F	S
1	2	3	4	5	6	7
8	9	10	11	12	13	14
15	16	17	18	19	20	21
22	23	24	25	26	27	28
29	30	31				

October

MONDAY

9 Yom Kippur
Thanksgiving Day

TUESDAY

10

WEDNESDAY

11 b.1861 Mary Ellen Smith, MLA, first woman cabinet minister in the British Empire

THURSDAY

12

FRIDAY ○

13

SATURDAY

14 Sukkoth
b.1887 Frances Loring, sculptor, co-founder of the Sculptors' Society of Canada and chief organizer of the
National Arts Council

SUNDAY

15

THE RESOURCEFULNESS OF WOMEN

There is no barren place in life that a woman cannot dress with her ingenuity—be it a state of mind or a state of being. She can come into a shack, put scraps of curtain at the window, crochet a mat or two out of rags, fill up the cracks with water-soaked newspaper, and proceed to be comfortable, even contented. If she lacks utensils, she will make a spoon out of kindling wood, a potato masher out of a rock and stick, and a cooking vessel out of an old tin can. She'll get something together, never fear. Most men in the same environment would half starve, half freeze, or half pity themselves to death.

from "The Chatelaine On Women's Resourcefulness" by Anne Elizabeth Wilson, April 1928

OCTOBER

S	M	T	W	T	F	S
1	2	3	4	5	6	7
8	9	10	11	12	13	14
15	16	17	18	19	20	21
22	23	24	25	26	27	28
29	30	31				

October

MONDAY

16

TUESDAY

17
d.1868 Laura Secord, heroine of the War of 1812

WEDNESDAY

18
Persons Day
1929 The British Privy Council decrees that Canadian women are "persons"

THURSDAY

19

FRIDAY ◑

20
b.1873 Nellie McClung, author, feminist and Alberta MLA 1921–1926

SATURDAY

21
Marguerite Bourgeoys, founder of the Congrégation des Filles séculières de Ville Marie in 1669, is canonized a saint by Pope John Paul II in 1982

SUNDAY

22

Emily Murphy, July 1929 issue

A WOMAN'S PLACE

Now that the Senate is (to indulge for a moment in a mis-quotation) to become a *place aux dames,* the question is asked, "What possibilities does it open for women?" The subject requires no deep or extensive inquiry such as Locke made into human understanding, for, after all, the answer is quite a simple one. The possibilities for women in the Senate are the same as exist for men.

from "Now that Women are Persons, What's Ahead?" by Emily Murphy, December 1929

When the Supreme Court of Canada ruled that women were not "persons" and therefore could not sit in the Senate, five Canadian women, including Judge Emily Murphy, successfully appealed their case before the British Privy Council.

OCTOBER

S	M	T	W	T	F	S
1	2	3	4	5	6	7
8	9	10	11	12	13	14
15	16	17	18	19	20	21
22	23	24	25	26	27	28
29	30	31				

Women and the War Effort

With the outbreak of the Second World War, the Department of National Defense began an aggressive advertising campaign in *Chatelaine* urging women to purchase Victory Bonds and to sign up for active duty. "Men shall not die because I faltered," was one of the slogans used. Women took jobs in munitions factories and machine shops; they joined the army, navy and air force; and voluntary groups sprang up all over the country training women in first aid, ambulance work and mechanics. By 1941 the Voluntary Registration of Canadian Women had enlisted over a quarter of a million women.

Although the war allowed women to make serious inroads into fields that were once exclusive to men, they were told again and again they were doing a "man's job" by serving their country. The implication was that the work was temporary.

Even as a temporary measure, women in uniforms and pants were a source of serious concern and, initially, widespread disapproval. Recruitment literature, commercial advertising and even *Chatelaine* articles were preoccupied with the lack of femininity of women in uniforms and coveralls and advised them to pay special attention to their appearance, as it was now essential for troop morale.

"Some folk have been 'viewing with alarm' the pronouncements of certain Government controllers forecasting 'no more of this' and 'no more of that' in the beauty preparation field. But really, no cause for worry at the moment. Surely the ingenuity of the beauty experts can be relied upon to produce substitute materials, where they're needed—to replace substances now required for war industry.

"One Dismal Desmond was trying to tell a crowd of soldier boys about potential shortages in beauty preparations. 'In another year there won't be any more of 'em,' he said. To which one bright youth retorted, 'Say, they can't do that to us. No more beautiful girls? What are we fighting for?'"

from "Beauty Brevities," January 1942

"During the war when there was feverish effort to pretend that women were equal to men, there were still no titles, except unimportant ones, no ribbons—except in the shops—for women. We were expected to give, and did give—the women of all nations—the tremendous enthusiasm, the sustained ideals of patriotism, even though sometimes misplaced, of which we are peculiarly capable."

from "Are Women Wanted in Public Life?" Helen Gregory MacGill, September 1928

OCTOBER

MONDAY

23 National Sisters' Day

TUESDAY

24

WEDNESDAY

25 1993 Fifty-three women are elected to the House of Commons

THURSDAY

26

FRIDAY ●

27 d.1933 Emily Murphy, author, first woman magistrate and appellant in the "Persons" case

SATURDAY

28 Last day of daylight saving time
1868 *The Globe* reports that 54 percent of Toronto inhabitants are female and 5,000 of them earn their own living

SUNDAY

29

BLAZING TRAILS

Elsie Gregory MacGill came from a long line of pioneering women. Her grandmother was an early fighter for women's suffrage; her mother, Helen Gregory MacGill, was one of Canada's first woman judges. So it was hardly surprising when Elsie started blazing some trails of her own. She was the first woman to receive the Gzowski award for engineering in recognition of her work designing the Hurricane Fighter. As Chief Engineer at the Canadian Car and Foundry's Fort William plant during the Second World War, she was responsible for the building of thousands of planes—one of the most vital operations of the Canadian war effort.

OCTOBER

S	M	T	W	T	F	S
1	2	3	4	5	6	7
8	9	10	11	12	13	14
15	16	17	18	19	20	21
22	23	24	25	26	27	28
29	30	31				

CHATELAINE

Ten Cents

NOVEMBER 194

Featuring a New Serial
"Thanks! Mr. Hitler" *By Enid J. Watts*

NOVEMBER

S	M	T	W	T	F	S
				1	2	3	4
5	6	7	8	9	10	11
12	13	14	15	16	17	18
19	20	21	22	23	24	25
26	27	28	29	30		

October/November

MONDAY

30

TUESDAY

31 Hallowe'en
d.1957 Mrs. George Black, second woman to sit in the House of Commons

WEDNESDAY

1 d.1931 Harriet Stewart, first woman in the British Empire to receive the degree of Bachelor of Arts (Mount Allison University, 1882)

THURSDAY

2

FRIDAY

3 1876 The Toronto Women's Literary Society is founded by Dr. Emily Stowe

SATURDAY ◑

4 d.1980 Elsie Gregory MacGill, aeronautical engineer

SUNDAY

5

November

MONDAY

6

TUESDAY

7

WEDNESDAY

8

THURSDAY

9
b.1873 Marie Dressler, Academy Award-winning Canadian actress

FRIDAY

10
b.1921 Doris Anderson, editor of *Chatelaine* from 1957 to 1977

SATURDAY ○

11
Remembrance Day
d.1932 Mrs. Georgina Alexandrina Newhall, journalist and first editor of the women's page in the *Toronto News*

SUNDAY

12
1991 June Rowlands becomes the first woman elected mayor of Toronto

May 1934 issue

THE WAVE OF FASHION

Have you had a fling at a high hair style? Maybe you've been wintering with it up? Whichever it is, change it. There's nothing like a brand-new hair-do to give you that youthful springtime feeling…and set a smart outfit off.

If you haven't yet tried those enchanting top-curls, see if you don't get yourself a completely new personality with them. Particularly on glamorous evenings with the soft and feminine 1939 dinner dresses.

from "The Promise of Beauty" by MAB, December 1941

NOVEMBER

S	M	T	W	T	F	S
				1	2	3	4
5	6	7	8	9	10	11
12	13	14	15	16	17	18
19	20	21	22	23	24	25
26	27	28	29	30		

November

MONDAY

13

TUESDAY

14

WEDNESDAY

15

THURSDAY

16

FRIDAY

17

SATURDAY ◗

18 b.1939 Margaret Atwood, author

SUNDAY

19

I RESOLVE...TO LOOK ATTRACTIVE
WHILE I WORK

At any moment fate may walk into my kitchen or my office. So I'm going to look my best all the time. When I go to the office, it's only fifteen minutes extra in morning make-up and dressing will repay me all throughout the day. Just starting with a pressed frock and laundered cuffs and collar, fresh lingerie and hose does something to my personality, it makes me surer of myself, more confident. And it's appreciated by my co-workers and chiefs. It's a good thing to remember, too, that business men go for black with white touches, and strong husbands weaken in the face of the little woman in a fresh gingham gown.

from "I Resolve..." January 1938

April 1943 issue

NOVEMBER

S	M	T	W	T	F	S
			1	2	3	4
5	6	7	8	9	10	11
12	13	14	15	16	17	18
19	20	21	22	23	24	25
26	27	28	29	30		

November

MONDAY

20

TUESDAY

21

WEDNESDAY

22

THURSDAY

23 American Thanksgiving Day

FRIDAY

24 b.1881 Florence Wyle, sculptor

SATURDAY ●

25 International Day to End Violence Against Women

SUNDAY

26

August 1929 issue

KIT COLEMAN

When the Spanish–American war broke out in 1898, Kit Coleman caught the first train to Washington and talked her way onto a freighter bound for Cuba. When she cabled her first story to the *Toronto Mail and Empire,* she became the world's first woman war correspondent. Born in Ireland, she came to Canada during the 1880s, when women were beginning to attend university and enter the professions. The *Toronto Mail and Empire* hired her to produce a page appealing to this "New Woman." Instead of filling it with fashion reports and gossip, as her editor suggested, Kit devoted the space to interviews, theatre reviews and political commentary. Her "Woman's Kingdom" section became so popular, it tripled in size within only a few months.

NOVEMBER

S	M	T	W	T	F	S
			1	2	3	4
5	6	7	8	9	10	11
12	13	14	15	16	17	18
19	20	21	22	23	24	25
26	27	28	29	30		

DECEMBER						
S	M	T	W	T	F	S
					1	2
3	4	5	6	7	8	9
10	11	12	13	14	15	16
17	18	19	20	21	22	23
24	25	26	27	28	29	30
31						

November/December

MONDAY

27 1980 The Canada Pension Plan is extended to housewives, on a voluntary basis

TUESDAY

28 d.1867 Julia Catherine Hart, author of *St. Ursula's Convent,* the first novel written by a Canadian in Canada

WEDNESDAY

29

THURSDAY

30 b.1874 Lucy Maud Montgomery, author

FRIDAY

1

SATURDAY

2 1989 Audrey McLaughlin is elected leader of the NDP, becoming the first woman to lead a federal political party

SUNDAY ◗

3

December

MONDAY

4   b.1945 Roberta Bondar, first Canadian woman in space

TUESDAY

5

WEDNESDAY

6   National Day of Remembrance and Action on Violence Against Women
b.1803 Susanna Moodie, author

THURSDAY

7

FRIDAY

8

SATURDAY

9   d.1980 Doris Winifred Nielsen, MP 1940–1945

SUNDAY

10   Human Rights Day
1948 The Universal Declaration of Human Rights is adopted and proclaimed by the UN General Assembly

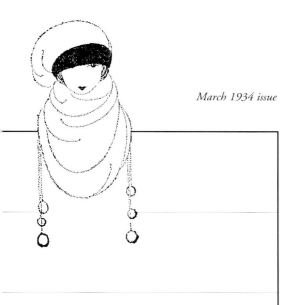

March 1934 issue

DECEMBER

S	M	T	W	T	F	S
					1	2
3	4	5	6	7	8	9
10	11	12	13	14	15	16
17	18	19	20	21	22	23
24	25	26	27	28	29	30
31						

THE PERFUME OF CHRISTMAS

The Christmas season brings to mind the aroma of perfume, perhaps because one of the first gifts to the Christ child included myrrh and frankincense. Reminiscent of worship, swinging censers and burning incense, there is no element of modern life more closely connected with the past and more redolent of romance than perfume. All through the ages perfume has been associated not only with feminine beauty, but with the ceremonies of practically every religion in the world. It is hardly surprising, therefore, that it should be considered one of the most fitting gifts at this festive season.

from "The Promise of Beauty" by MAB, December 1929

THE HOLIDAY SEASON

There's nothing like planning for the holiday Christmas season, a time to rejoice with family, friends and good food. *Chatelaine* never stinted on advice for the holidays and was always sure to offer suggestions on everything from etiquette when attending your in-laws' holiday dinner to planning and preparing for your own. Take a peek at a few of these festive holiday ideas.

"Write 'apples' on your Christmas shopping list; it's just as blessed to give as to receive them. Eating apples is a matter of patriotism to our country as well as profit and pleasure to ourselves. Smart folks do tricks with apples to make the hearth, the window or the table a thing of beauty and a joy forever. Here they are in a Christmas wreath—spruce, cedar, pine, all mixed together as a background for pine cones, crimson apples and scarlet holly berries. Hang it over the mantel or in a window. Or some other spot where it will do a lot of good, decoratively speaking."

from "Apples for Decoration," December 1939

CHRISTMAS IDEA

No summer garlands ever provided half the fun and merriment that arises out of the stringing of popcorn and cranberry garlands for the tree. Yards and yards of cranberries will wind themselves round the tree, contrasting its rich greenery with their equally rich red.

BIRD NOTES—HOW TO CHOOSE

"Chicken, duck, goose or a noble turkey? Well that's up to you; it's your Christmas dinner. But you'd better consider the question from all its angles—the size of your party and your oven, the state of your pocketbook, and the family tradition in the matter, and what bird you like best on your platter. A twelve-pound turkey as purchased serves sixteen once round, but you'll probably have to count on seconds for everyone. If it's chicken, a five-pounder will look after six holiday appetites. A duck of this same weight goes only far enough for four people, and a nine- or ten-pound goose is about right for six. So count noses and govern yourself accordingly."

from "Bird Notes," December 1939

December

MONDAY ○

11

TUESDAY

12

WEDNESDAY

13 b.1871 Emily Carr, painter and author

THURSDAY

14

FRIDAY

15

SATURDAY

16

SUNDAY ◑

17

January 1933 issue

DECEMBER

S	M	T	W	T	F	S
					1	2
3	4	5	6	7	8	9
10	11	12	13	14	15	16
17	18	19	20	21	22	23
24	25	26	27	28	29	30
31						

SNOW-SHOES AND SNOW LADIES

When Grandma was a girl, snowdrifts meant settling down to a long winter's embroidery. She snuggled into extra warm petticoats and a cosy delaine and threw another log on the fire. Outdoors was a man's world! Today's girls live the rich, full outdoor life…they've mastered the wind and storm of the Great Canadian Winter and they glory in it. *Chatelaine* often offered advice on the rigours of Canadian winters for its readers. Now, the lithe, graceful, feminine figures skim over snow and ice without a worry. Neither the clothes nor the wearers show evidence of limpness or fatigue after a day on the hills. Canadian girls have mastered the demanding beauty regimen of a chameleon-like complexion.

December

MONDAY

18

TUESDAY

19

WEDNESDAY

20

THURSDAY

21

FRIDAY

22 First day of Hanukkah

SATURDAY

23 1983 Jeanne Sauvé is the first woman appointed governor-general

SUNDAY

24 Christmas Eve

August 1935 issue

LEARN TO BE ADMIRED
CHATELAINE SERVICE BULLETINS
ON BEAUTY CULTURE

Not twenty women out of a hundred know how to make up effectively. Some overdo it; others use the wrong materials. Yet the right make-up can give a plain face charm, a lovely face character. Learn the secrets of make-up, of high-lighting, of facial structure, of color and texture selection. Learn how to stress your best features and make the least of your worst. Learn about the make-up which is individually yours. Price 10 cents. Order by number from Chatelaine Service Bulletins.

BEAUTIFUL HANDS	A LOVELY SKIN
Bulletin No. 15 5 cents	Bulletin No. 18 10 cents

HOW TO BE FRESH AS A FLOWER
Bulletin No. 19 5 cents

from "Chatelaine Service Bulletins" advertisement, August 1935

DECEMBER

S	M	T	W	T	F	S
					1	2
3	4	5	6	7	8	9
10	11	12	13	14	15	16
17	18	19	20	21	22	23
24	25	26	27	28	29	30
31						

December

MONDAY ●

25 Christmas Day

TUESDAY

26 Boxing Day

WEDNESDAY

27

THURSDAY

28

FRIDAY

29

SATURDAY

30

SUNDAY

31 New Year's Eve
b.1884 Florence Nightingale Graham, the Canadian woman who became Elizabeth Arden

April 1929 issue

CHATELAINE'S GUIDING LIGHT

In her first issue, The Chatelaine set her lamp in the window and found that it cast a long light. Her lamp, burning steadily, has proved a certain beacon through the year to thousands of Canadian women. Through those "immortal" years to which we look forward, we hope that it will continue to throw always that living beam.

from "As Seen from a Four-Poster" by Anne Elizabeth Wilson, February 1929

DECEMBER

S	M	T	W	T	F	S
					1	2
3	4	5	6	7	8	9
10	11	12	13	14	15	16
17	18	19	20	21	22	23
24	25	26	27	28	29	30
31						

The Millennium

The twentieth century has been one of firsts for Canadian women. From the first woman MP to the first woman in space, women have blazed new trails and made a place for themselves in almost every area of human pursuit. They have fought for local hospitals and good schools for their children; for equal pay and equality under the eyes of the law; for justice and for peace. And now, at the close of the twentieth century, many of those dreams have finally been realized.

Our victories have been myriad and hard won. We now count women in the ranks of Canada's cabinet ministers and CEOs, union leaders and university professors, firefighters and chiefs of police, mega-selling performers and elite athletes. But the success of one woman, even today, is a breakthrough for all.

There is still a long way to go. Woman earn only about seventy cents to a man's dollar; one in four women will be sexually assaulted in her lifetime; thousands of Canadian women and children live in poverty, and we all live in the shadows of the greenhouse effect, cancer and AIDS.

Let's hope the twenty-first century will bring an end to "firsts" for women. Women in Canada and the world over will take a second, third and thousandth helping of success. As they meet the challenges the new century offers, they will remember their mothers and grandmothers who helped to clear the way so they might flourish.

Mary Craig McGeachy, the first woman diplomat in the British Empire

Alice Jamieson—she and Emily Murphy were Canada's first woman magistrates

An early suffragist

Mary Ellen Smith, first president of the National Federation of Liberal Women of Canada

HAPPY NEW YEAR

Only Twenty-Five Years Ago!
June 1909, women of the world, meeting at the International
Council of Women were working feverishly for such things as
Votes for women
Women delegates to school boards
Supervised playgrounds
Medical inspection of schools
Appointment of school nurses
Pasteurization of milk
To-day we take these for granted

from "At the International Council of Women," November 1934

POLITICAL MILESTONES FOR CANADIAN WOMEN

1916 Emily Murphy and Alice Jamieson are the first women to be appointed police magistrates in the British Empire

1921 Agnes MacPhail becomes the first woman member of Parliament

1929 The Famous Five win their appeal to the British Privy Council and Canadian women are declared "persons"

1930 Cairine Wilson is the first woman to be appointed to the Senate

1957 Ellen Fairclough becomes the first female cabinet minister

1962 Claire Kirkland-Casgrain becomes the first female to serve in the Quebec cabinet

1972 Muriel Ferguson becomes the first woman to be appointed Speaker of the Senate

1974 Pauline McGibbon is appointed the first woman lieutenant-governor of Ontario

1980 Jeanne Sauvé is elected the first woman Speaker of the House of Commons

1982 Bertha Wilson is the first woman to be appointed to the Supreme Court

1989 Audrey McLaughlin becomes the first female federal leader

1991 Rita Johnson becomes the first woman provincial premier

1993 Catherine Callbeck is the first woman to be elected premier

1993 Kim Campbell becomes the first woman prime minister

Agnes MacPhail, Canada's first woman MP

NOTES

Family Tree

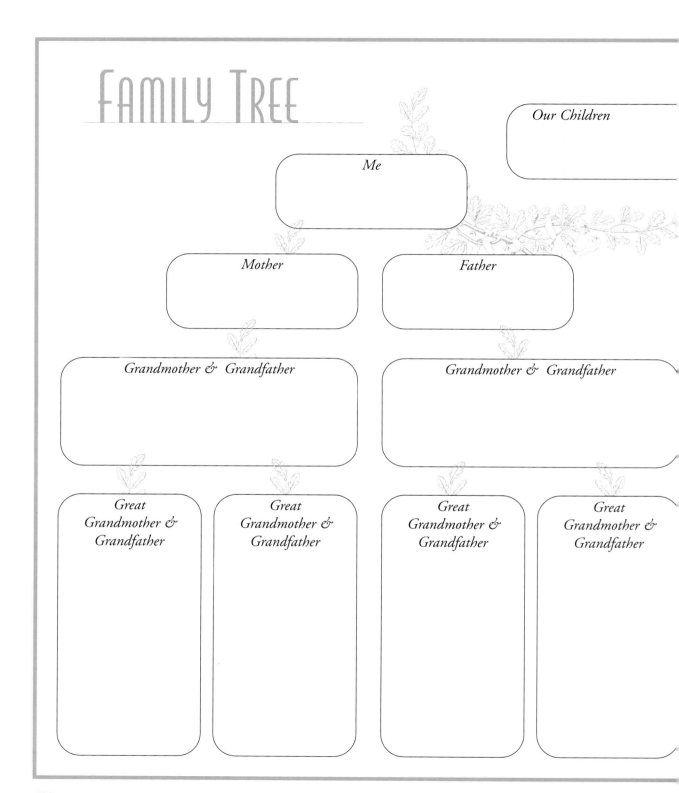

Our Children

Me

Mother

Father

Grandmother & Grandfather

Grandmother & Grandfather

Great Grandmother & Grandfather

Great Grandmother & Grandfather

Great Grandmother & Grandfather

Great Grandmother & Grandfather

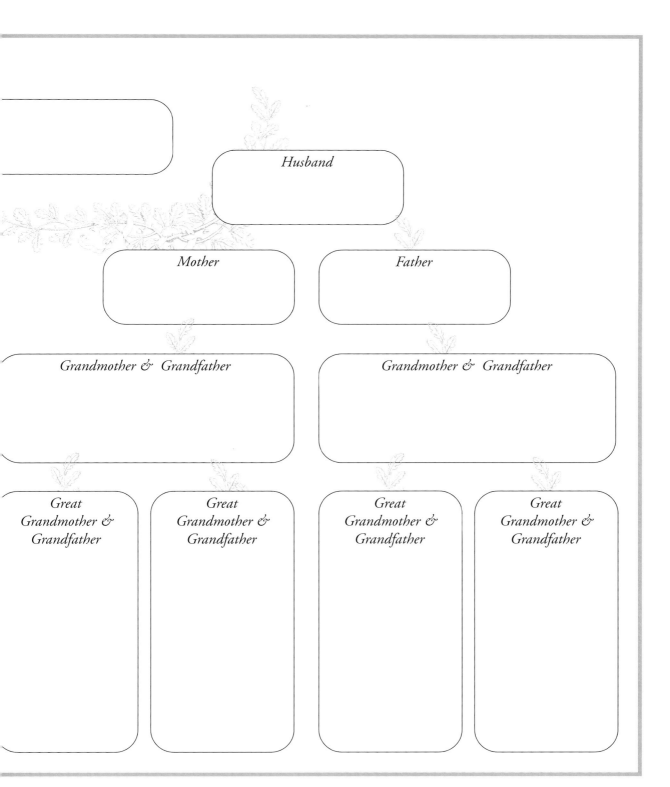

Husband

Mother

Father

Grandmother & Grandfather

Grandmother & Grandfather

Great
Grandmother &
Grandfather

Great
Grandmother &
Grandfather

Great
Grandmother &
Grandfather

Great
Grandmother &
Grandfather

BIRTHDAYS

MONTH	NAME & DATE	MONTH	NAME & DATE
January		July	
February		August	
March		September	
April		October	
May		November	
June		December	

Emergency Numbers

POLICE _____

FIRE _____

AMBULANCE _____

LOCAL POLICE STATION _____

DOCTOR _____

DENTIST _____

PEDIATRICIAN _____

PHARMACY _____

VET _____

GARAGE _____

PLUMBER _____

ELECTRICIAN _____

GAS _____

WATER _____

SCHOOL _____

BABY-SITTER _____

GRANDPARENTS _____

GRANDPARENTS _____

OFFICE _____

HAIRDRESSER _____

_____

_____

_____

_____

Addresses

NAME AND ADDRESS	TELEPHONE/FAX/E-MAIL

NAME AND ADDRESS   TELEPHONE/FAX/E-MAIL

NAME AND ADDRESS   TELEPHONE/FAX/E-MAIL

NAME AND ADDRESS

TELEPHONE/FAX/E-MAIL

Predictions for the Year 2001

To celebrate the new millennium, try making a few predictions for the year (and the century) to come. You can check this time capsule full of your hopes, plans and dreams next year—and see whether your prophecies were fulfilled.

MY PREDICTIONS

For me:

For my family:

For my friends:

For the rich and famous:

In the news:

In politics:

2000

JANUARY
S	M	T	W	T	F	S
						1
2	3	4	5	6	7	8
9	10	11	12	13	14	15
16	17	18	19	20	21	22
23	24	25	26	27	28	29
30	31					

FEBRUARY
S	M	T	W	T	F	S
		1	2	3	4	5
6	7	8	9	10	11	12
13	14	15	16	17	18	19
20	21	22	23	24	25	26
27	28	29				

MARCH
S	M	T	W	T	F	S
			1	2	3	4
5	6	7	8	9	10	11
12	13	14	15	16	17	18
19	20	21	22	23	24	25
26	27	28	29	30	31	

APRIL
S	M	T	W	T	F	S
						1
2	3	4	5	6	7	8
9	10	11	12	13	14	15
16	17	18	19	20	21	22
23	24	25	26	27	28	29
30						

MAY
S	M	T	W	T	F	S
	1	2	3	4	5	6
7	8	9	10	11	12	13
14	15	16	17	18	19	20
21	22	23	24	25	26	27
28	29	30	31			

JUNE
S	M	T	W	T	F	S
				1	2	3
4	5	6	7	8	9	10
11	12	13	14	15	16	17
18	19	20	21	22	23	24
25	26	27	28	29	30	

JULY
S	M	T	W	T	F	S
						1
2	3	4	5	6	7	8
9	10	11	12	13	14	15
16	17	18	19	20	21	22
23	24	25	26	27	28	29
30	31					

AUGUST
S	M	T	W	T	F	S
		1	2	3	4	5
6	7	8	9	10	11	12
13	14	15	16	17	18	19
20	21	22	23	24	25	26
27	28	29	30	31		

SEPTEMBER
S	M	T	W	T	F	S
					1	2
3	4	5	6	7	8	9
10	11	12	13	14	15	16
17	18	19	20	21	22	23
24	25	26	27	28	29	30

OCTOBER
S	M	T	W	T	F	S
1	2	3	4	5	6	7
8	9	10	11	12	13	14
15	16	17	18	19	20	21
22	23	24	25	26	27	28
29	30	31				

NOVEMBER
S	M	T	W	T	F	S
			1	2	3	4
5	6	7	8	9	10	11
12	13	14	15	16	17	18
19	20	21	22	23	24	25
26	27	28	29	30		

DECEMBER
S	M	T	W	T	F	S
					1	2
3	4	5	6	7	8	9
10	11	12	13	14	15	16
17	18	19	20	21	22	23
24	25	26	27	28	29	30
31						

2001

JANUARY
S	M	T	W	T	F	S
	1	2	3	4	5	6
7	8	9	10	11	12	13
14	15	16	17	18	19	20
21	22	23	24	25	26	27
28	29	30	31			

FEBRUARY
S	M	T	W	T	F	S
				1	2	3
4	5	6	7	8	9	10
11	12	13	14	15	16	17
18	19	20	21	22	23	24
25	26	27	28			

MARCH
S	M	T	W	T	F	S
				1	2	3
4	5	6	7	8	9	10
11	12	13	14	15	16	17
18	19	20	21	22	23	24
25	26	27	28	29	30	31

APRIL
S	M	T	W	T	F	S
1	2	3	4	5	6	7
8	9	10	11	12	13	14
15	16	17	18	19	20	21
22	23	24	25	26	27	28
29	30					

MAY
S	M	T	W	T	F	S
		1	2	3	4	5
6	7	8	9	10	11	12
13	14	15	16	17	18	19
20	21	22	23	24	25	26
27	28	29	30	31		

JUNE
S	M	T	W	T	F	S
					1	2
3	4	5	6	7	8	9
10	11	12	13	14	15	16
17	18	19	20	21	22	23
24	25	26	27	28	29	30

JULY
S	M	T	W	T	F	S
1	2	3	4	5	6	7
8	9	10	11	12	13	14
15	16	17	18	19	20	21
22	23	24	25	26	27	28
29	30	31				

AUGUST
S	M	T	W	T	F	S
			1	2	3	4
5	6	7	8	9	10	11
12	13	14	15	16	17	18
19	20	21	22	23	24	25
26	27	28	29	30	31	

SEPTEMBER
S	M	T	W	T	F	S
						1
2	3	4	5	6	7	8
9	10	11	12	13	14	15
16	17	18	19	20	21	22
23	24	25	26	27	28	29
30						

OCTOBER
S	M	T	W	T	F	S
	1	2	3	4	5	6
7	8	9	10	11	12	13
14	15	16	17	18	19	20
21	22	23	24	25	26	27
28	29	30	31			

NOVEMBER
S	M	T	W	T	F	S
				1	2	3
4	5	6	7	8	9	10
11	12	13	14	15	16	17
18	19	20	21	22	23	24
25	26	27	28	29	30	

DECEMBER
S	M	T	W	T	F	S
						1
2	3	4	5	6	7	8
9	10	11	12	13	14	15
16	17	18	19	20	21	22
23	24	25	26	27	28	29
30	31					

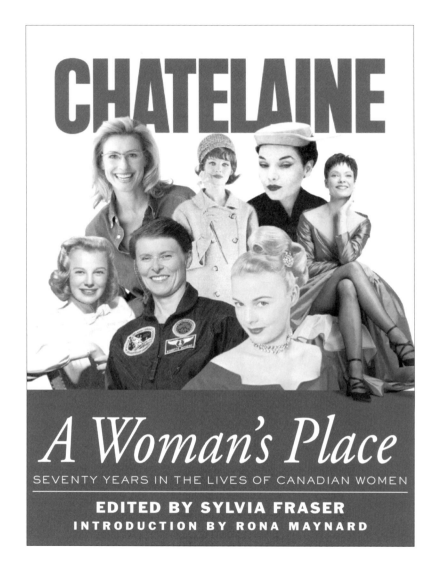

CHATELAINE

A Woman's Place

SEVENTY YEARS IN THE LIVES OF CANADIAN WOMEN

EDITED BY SYLVIA FRASER
INTRODUCTION BY RONA MAYNARD

The

CHATELAINE DAYBOOK

2000